HMH Florida Science

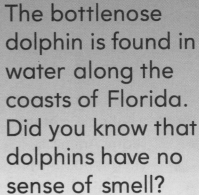

Acknowledgment for cover and title page: ©Andrea Izzotti/Shutterstock

Florida Standards courtesy of the Florida Department of Education.

Printed in the U.S.A.

ISBN   978-1-328-79355-3

7 8 9 10   0877   26 25 24 23 22 21

4500819182   B C D E F G

The bottlenose dolphin is found in water along the coasts of Florida. Did you know that dolphins have no sense of smell?

Houghton Mifflin Harcourt

Contents

Our Senses

touch

smell

hear

see

taste

SC.K.N.1.1 Collaborate with a partner to collect information. **SC.K.N.1.2** Make observations of the natural world and know that they are descriptors collected using the five senses. **SC.K.N.1.3** Keep records as appropriate — such as pictorial records — of investigations conducted. **SC.K.N.1.4** Observe and create a visual representation of an object which includes its major features. **SC.K.N.1.5** Recognize that learning can come from careful observation. **SC.K.L.14.1** Recognize the five senses and related body parts. (TE) **HE.K.C.1.5** Recognize there are body parts inside and outside of the body. (TE)

Name _____

see

hear

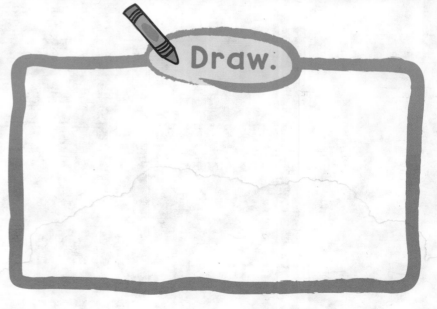

Draw.

Your senses help you learn.
You see things with your eyes.
You hear sounds with your ears.

▶ Draw something you see.

Name _____

touch

smell

taste

You touch things with your hands and skin.
You smell things with your nose.
You taste foods with your mouth.

▶ Circle the body part the girl is using to smell the flower.

Sum It Up!

● Circle the child hearing something. ▲ Circle the child seeing something. ■ Circle the child tasting something.

Science Skills

observe

compare

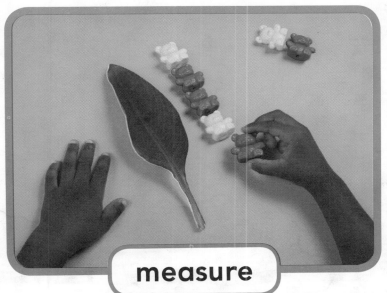

measure

big   small

sort

 SC.K.N.1.1 Collaborate…to collect information. **SC.K.N.1.2** Make observations of the natural world…using the five senses. **SC.K.N.1.3** Keep records as appropriate…of investigations conducted. **SC.K.N.1.4** Observe and create a visual representation of an object… **SC.K.N.1.5** Recognize that learning can come from careful observation. **SC.K.P.8.1** Sort objects by observable properties, such as size, shape, color, temperature (hot or cold), weight (heavy or light) and texture. (TE)

Name _____

observe

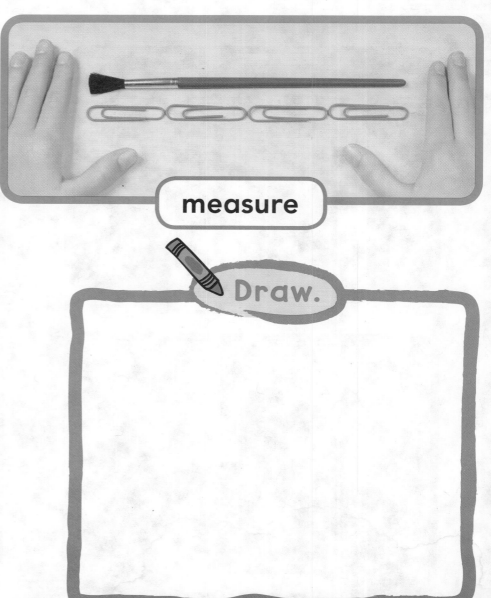

measure

Draw.

We ask questions to learn.
We observe to find answers.
We measure to find answers.

▶ Observe your hand. Draw what you observe.

Name _____

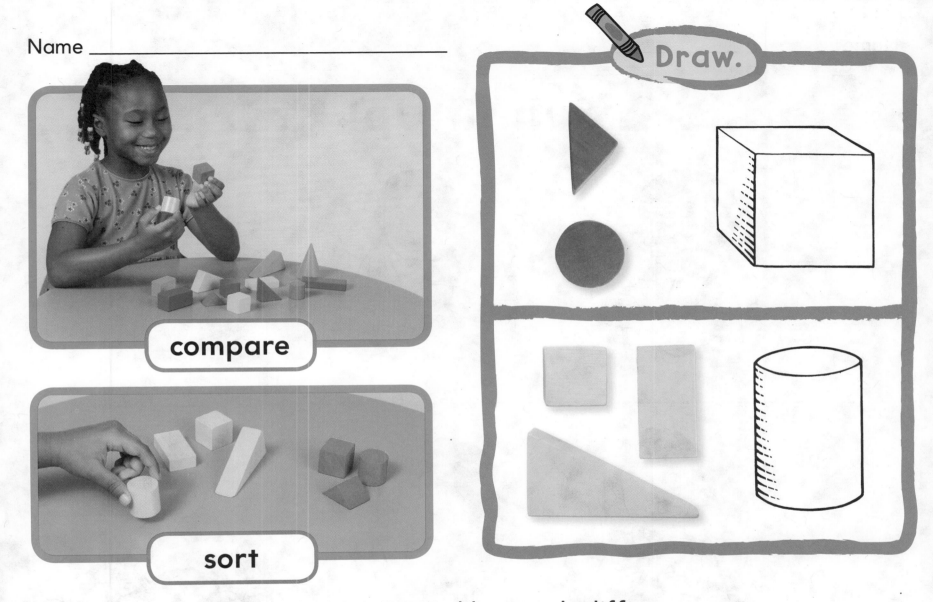

compare

sort

We compare how things are alike and different.
We sort things that are alike into groups.

► Color each block to match its group.

Sum It Up!

● Circle the child measuring something.
▲ Circle the child sorting things.

Science Tools

hand lens

thermometer

balance

measuring cup

ruler

SC.K.N.1.1 Collaborate with a partner to collect information. **SC.K.N.1.2** Make observations of the natural world and know that they are descriptors collected using the five senses. **SC.K.N.1.3** Keep records as appropriate — such as pictorial records — of investigations conducted. **SC.K.N.1.4** Observe and create a visual representation of an object which includes its major features. **SC.K.N.1.5** Recognize that learning can come from careful observation. (TE)

Name _____

hand lens

ruler

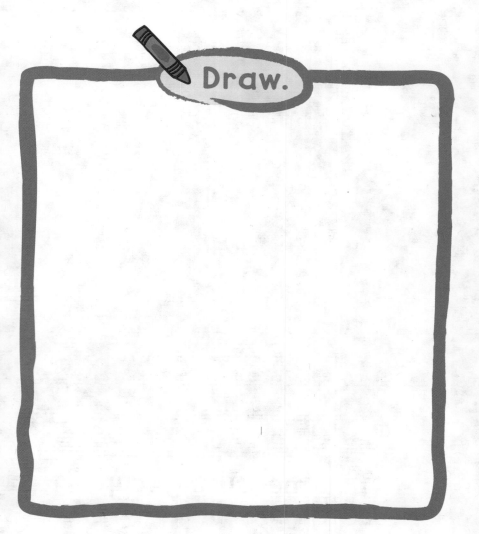

Draw.

We use science tools to learn about things.
A hand lens makes things look bigger.
A ruler can show how long something is.

Unit 1 • Lesson 3 •
How Do We Use Science Tools?

▶ Draw something you can measure with a ruler.

Name _____

balance

thermometer

measuring cup

A balance shows which thing is heavier.

A thermometer shows how warm it is.

A measuring cup shows how much water.

▶ Circle the thermometer.

Sum It Up!

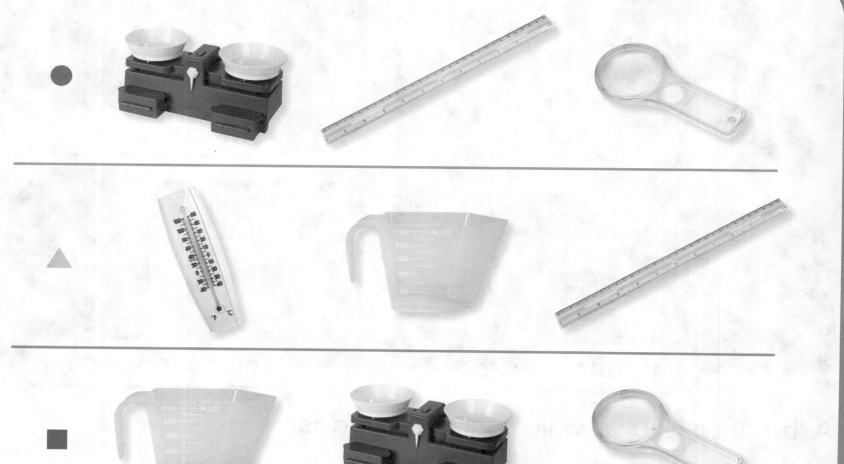

● Circle the ruler.   Circle the measuring cup.
■ Circle the hand lens.

Solving Problems

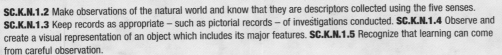

engineer

SC.K.N.1.2 Make observations of the natural world and know that they are descriptors collected using the five senses. **SC.K.N.1.3** Keep records as appropriate – such as pictorial records – of investigations conducted. **SC.K.N.1.4** Observe and create a visual representation of an object which includes its major features. **SC.K.N.1.5** Recognize that learning can come from careful observation.

Name _____

Engineers solve problems.
They design buildings and roads.
They design things we use at home.

▶ Draw a circle around the engineers.

Name _____

You can design things too.

Draw.

▶ Identify and explain what the child's problem might be. Discuss what he can do. Draw what the boy might design and build with the blocks.

Name _____

Unit 1 • Lesson 4 •
How Do Engineers Solve Problems?

Draw lines to match each problem to how an engineer solved the problem.

Design Process

problem

design

solve

SC.K.N.1.1 Collaborate with a partner to collect information. SC.K.N.1.2 Make observations of the natural world and know that they are descriptors collected using the five senses. SC.K.N.1.5 Recognize that learning can come from careful observation.

Name _____

Find a problem.

The design process is a plan with steps.
The steps can help you solve a problem.
The first step is to find a problem.

▶ Identify and explain the problem. Circle the problem.

Name _____

Please put litter here.

Plan and build.

Think of a way to solve the problem.
Design a plan. Then build it.

▶ Identify the girl's solution to the problem. Circle it.

Name _____

Test.

Improve.

Test your plan.

Does your plan solve the problem?

Can you make your plan better?

▶ Tell how the girl improved her plan.

Name _____

Redesign. Talk about it.

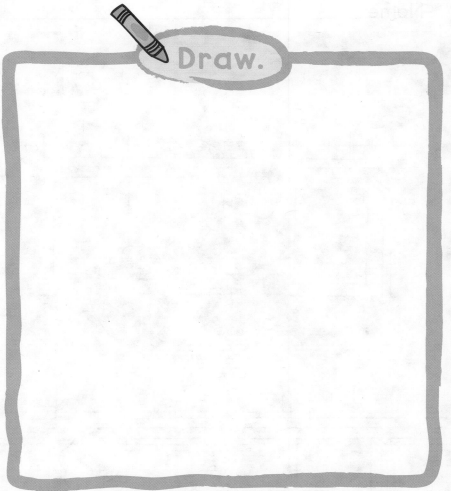

Draw.

Change your plan to make it better.
Talk with others about it.

▶ Think of another solution to the girl's problem. Draw a picture of it.
Explain your solution in your own words.

Name _____

Sum It Up!

The steps are not in order. Draw a line under the first step of the design process. Circle the last step of the design process.

Living and Nonliving

living things

nonliving things

SC.K.N.1.1 Collaborate with a partner to collect information. **SC.K.N.1.2** Make observations of the natural world and know that they are descriptors collected using the five senses. **SC.K.N.1.3** Keep records as appropriate — such as pictorial records — of investigations conducted. **SC.K.N.1.4** Observe and create a visual representation of an object which includes its major features. **SC.K.N.1.5** Recognize that learning can come from careful observation. **SC.K.L.14.3** Observe plants and animals, describe how they are alike and how they are different in the way they look and in the things they do. (TE)

Name _____

water

food

place to live

Living things need food and water.
They also need a place to live.
Do nonliving things need these?

▶ Circle the living thing getting food.

Name _____

new plant

ducks

Draw.

Plants can make more plants.
Animals can have young.
Can nonliving things do this?

▶ Draw a dog and its puppy.

Name _____

Sum It Up!

Unit 2 • Lesson 6 •
What Are Living Things?

● Circle the living thing.　▲ Circle the nonliving thing.

Real and Pretend

real

pretend

SC.K.N.1.1 Collaborate...to collect information. **SC.K.N.1.2** Make observations of the natural world...using the five senses. **SC.K.N.1.3** Keep records as appropriate — such as pictorial records — of investigations conducted. **SC.K.N.1.4** Observe and create a visual representation of an object which includes its major features. **SC.K.N.1.5** Recognize that learning can come from careful observation. **SC.K.L.14.2** Recognize that some books and other media portray animals and plants with characteristics and behaviors they do not have in real life. (TE)

Unit 2 • Lesson 7 •
What Is Real? What Is Pretend?

27

Name _____

real

pretend

Draw.

Pretend animals can do things real animals can not do.

▶ Draw a real animal.

Name _____

pretend

Draw.

Pretend plants can do things real plants can not do.

▶ Draw a real plant.

Unit 2 • Lesson 7 •
What Is Real? What Is Pretend?

29

Sum It Up!

● Circle the real thing.
▲ Circle the pretend thing.

Many Animals

fur

feathers

scales

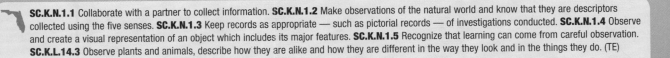

SC.K.N.1.1 Collaborate with a partner to collect information. **SC.K.N.1.2** Make observations of the natural world and know that they are descriptors collected using the five senses. **SC.K.N.1.3** Keep records as appropriate — such as pictorial records — of investigations conducted. **SC.K.N.1.4** Observe and create a visual representation of an object which includes its major features. **SC.K.N.1.5** Recognize that learning can come from careful observation. **SC.K.L.14.3** Observe plants and animals, describe how they are alike and how they are different in the way they look and in the things they do. (TE)

Name _____

blue jay

ladybug

elephant

Animals have different shapes and sizes.
Some animals have bright colors.

Unit 2 • Lesson 8 •
What Are Animals Like?

▶ Circle the blue animal. Draw a line under the smallest animal.

Name _____

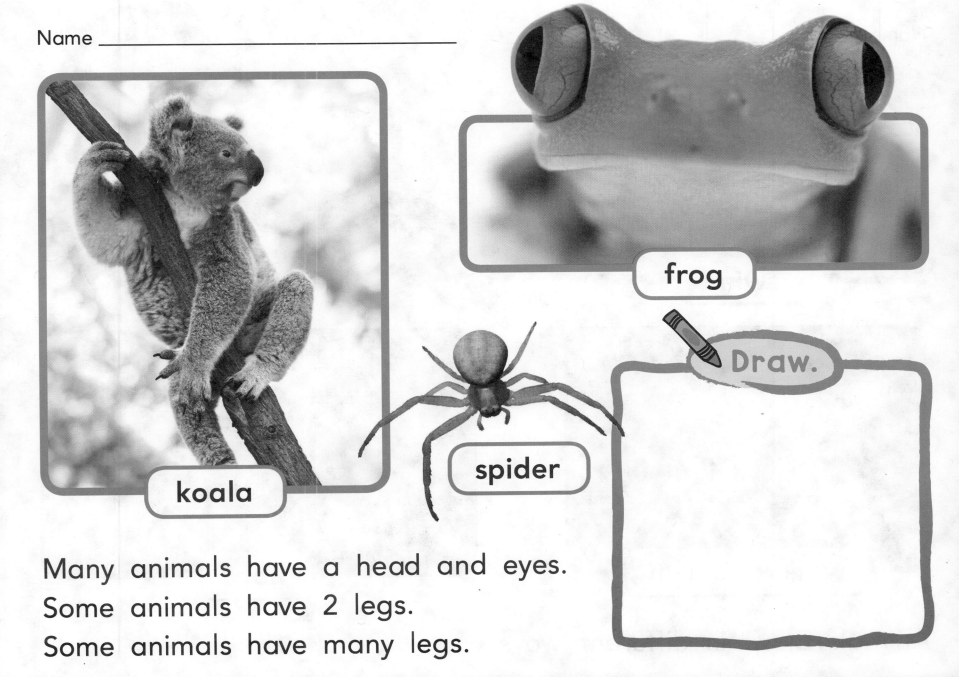

frog

koala

spider

Draw.

Many animals have a head and eyes.
Some animals have 2 legs.
Some animals have many legs.

▶ Draw the head and eyes of an animal.

swim

crawl

walk and run

hop

Animals move in different ways.

▶ Circle the animal that crawls.

Name _____

fly

Which animal hops?

Which animal swims?

Which animal walks and runs?

Draw.

▶ Draw an animal that flies.

Name _____

Sum It Up!

● Circle the animal that has fur. ▲ Circle the animal that swims. ■ Circle the animal that flies.

What Animals Need

food

air

water

shelter

SC.K.N.1.1 Collaborate with a partner to collect information. **SC.K.N.1.2** Make observations of the natural world and know that they are descriptors collected using the five senses. **SC.K.N.1.3** Keep records as appropriate — such as pictorial records — of investigations conducted. **SC.K.N.1.4** Observe and create a visual representation of an object which includes its major features. **SC.K.N.1.5** Recognize that learning can come from careful observation. **SC.K.L.14.3** Observe plants and animals, describe how they are alike and how they are different in the way they look and in the things they do. (TE)

Name _____

shelter

water

food

Animals need food, water, and air — just like you.
Animals need shelter — just like you.

▶ Circle the bear getting food.

Name _____

food

Draw.

Pets need people to give them food, water, and shelter.

▶ Draw a pet getting food and water.

Sum It Up!

Circle the things the squirrel needs.

Animals Grow and Change

life cycle

SC.K.N.1.1 Collaborate…to collect information. **SC.K.N.1.2** Make observations of the natural world…using the five senses.
SC.K.N.1.3 Keep records as appropriate — such as pictorial records — of investigations conducted. **SC.K.N.1.4** Observe and create
a visual representation of an object…. **SC.K.N.1.5** Recognize that learning can come from careful observation. **SC.K.L.14.3** Observe
plants and animals, describe how they are alike and how they are different in the way they look and in the things they do. (TE)

Name _____

month-old duckling

hatchling duck

adult duck

Animals change as they grow.

► Circle the hatchling duck.

Name _____

frog eggs

tadpole with 2 legs

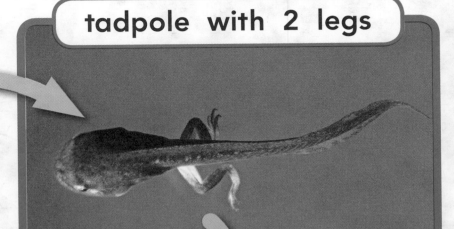

adult frog

tadpole with 4 legs

▶ Circle the adult frog.

Sum It Up!

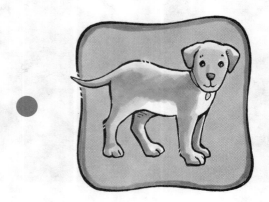  

How Do Animals Grow and Change?

● Circle the adult dog.
▲ Circle the newborn horse.

Many Plants

grass

tree

shrub

SC.K.N.1.1 Collaborate with a partner to collect information. **SC.K.N.1.2** Make observations of the natural world and know that they are descriptors collected using the five senses. **SC.K.N.1.3** Keep records as appropriate — such as pictorial records — of investigations conducted. **SC.K.N.1.4** Observe and create a visual representation of an object which includes its major features. **SC.K.N.1.5** Recognize that learning can come from careful observation. **SC.K.L.14.3** Observe plants and animals, describe how they are alike and how they are different in the way they look and in the things they do. (TE)

Name _____

trees

Trees, grasses, and shrubs are plants.
There are many kinds of trees.

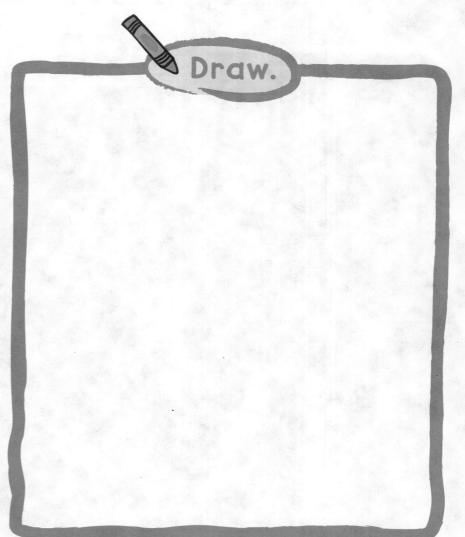

▶ Draw a tree.

Name _____

grasses

shrubs

There are many kinds of grasses.
There are many kinds of shrubs.

▶ Circle the tall grass.

Name _____

Sum It Up!

● Circle the tree. ▲ Circle the shrub.

What Plants Need

light

air

space to grow

soil

water

 SC.K.N.1.1 Collaborate with a partner to collect information. **SC.K.N.1.2** Make observations of the natural world and know that they are descriptors collected using the five senses. **SC.K.N.1.3** Keep records as appropriate — such as pictorial records — of investigations conducted. **SC.K.N.1.4** Observe and create a visual representation of an object which includes its major features. **SC.K.N.1.5** Recognize that learning can come from careful observation. **SC.K.L.14.3** Observe plants and animals, describe how they are alike and how they are different in the way they look and in the things they do. (TE)

Name _____

water   no water

Draw.

Plants need air, light, and water to live.

▶ Draw a plant getting water.

Name _____

space to grow

soil

Plants need soil.
Plants need space to grow.

▶ Most plants get the light they need from the sun. Draw the sun.

© Houghton Mifflin Harcourt Publishing Company © Richard Gross/Corbis

Sum It Up!

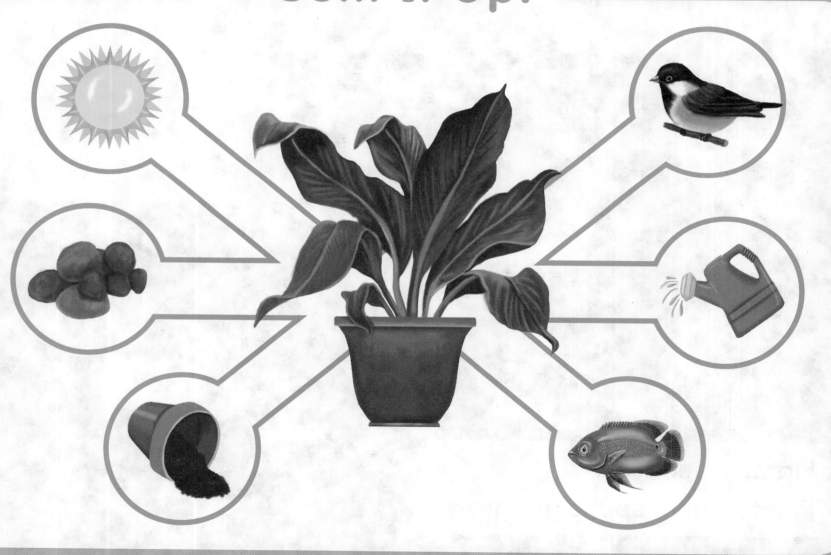

Draw a line to each thing the plant needs.

Plant Parts

leaf

flower

fruit

roots

seeds

stem

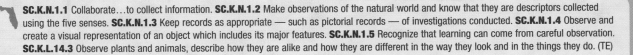

SC.K.N.1.1 Collaborate…to collect information. **SC.K.N.1.2** Make observations of the natural world and know that they are descriptors collected using the five senses. **SC.K.N.1.3** Keep records as appropriate — such as pictorial records — of investigations conducted. **SC.K.N.1.4** Observe and create a visual representation of an object which includes its major features. **SC.K.N.1.5** Recognize that learning can come from careful observation. **SC.K.L.14.3** Observe plants and animals, describe how they are alike and how they are different in the way they look and in the things they do. (TE)

Name _____

leaves

flowers

Draw.

Plants are made up of parts.
There are many kinds of leaves and flowers.

▶ Draw a leaf in the top box. Draw a flower in the bottom box.

Name _____

seeds

© Houghton Mifflin Harcourt Publishing Company   (t) ©Martin Bennett/Alamy; (c) ©Ryan Mcvay/Getty Images; (b) ©foodfolio/Alamy

Draw.

Fruit grows from the flowers of some plants.
Seeds grow in the fruit.

▶ Draw a fruit.

Sum It Up!

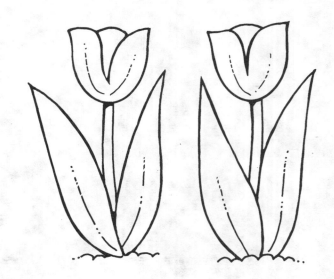

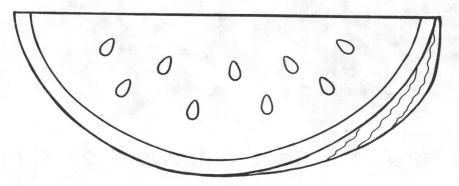

Color the roots brown. Color the stems and leaves green.
Color the flowers yellow. Color the fruit red. Color the seeds black.

Plants Grow and Change

seed

flower

sprout

seedling

adult plant

SC.K.N.1.1 Collaborate… to collect information. **SC.K.N.1.2** Make observations of the natural world… using the five senses.
SC.K.N.1.3 Keep records as appropriate… of investigations conducted. **SC.K.N.1.4** Observe and create a visual representation of an
object which includes its major features. **SC.K.N.1.5** Recognize that learning can come from careful observation. **SC.K.L.14.3** Observe
plants and animals, describe how they are alike and how they are different in the way they look and in the things they do. (TE)

Name _____

seed

sprout

seedling

A plant has a life cycle.
A plant changes as it grows.

▶ Circle the seed.

Name _____

Draw.

young tree

adult tree

▶ Draw a young tree.

Name _____

Sum It Up!

Circle the sprout. Draw a line under the adult tree.

Day Sky

sky

sun

clouds

SC.K.N.1.1 Collaborate…to collect information. **SC.K.N.1.2** Make observations of the natural world…. **SC.K.N.1.3** Keep records…. **SC.K.N.1.4** Observe and create a visual representation…. **SC.K.N.1.5** Recognize that learning can come from careful observation. **SC.K.E.5.1** Explore the Law of Gravity…. **SC.K.E.5.2** Recognize…day and night. **SC.K.E.5.3** Recognize that the Sun can only be seen in the daytime. **SC.K.E.5.5** Observe that things can be big and things can be small as seen from Earth. **SC.K.E.5.6** Observe that some objects are far away and some are nearby as seen from Earth. (TE)

Unit 4 • Lesson 15 •
What Is in the Day Sky?

61

Name _____

morning

noon

afternoon

We see the sun in the sky during the day.

We also see clouds and other objects in the sky.

During the day, the sun seems to move across the sky.

▶ Circle the sun in each picture.

Name _____

far

Draw.

near

Objects near Earth look big.
Objects far from Earth look small.

▶ Draw the sky during the day.

Sum It Up!

● Circle the sun in the morning.
▲ Circle the sun in the middle of the day.
■ Circle the sun in the afternoon.

Night Sky

stars

moon

SC.K.N.1.1 Collaborate…to collect information. **SC.K.N.1.2** Make observations…. **SC.K.N.1.3** Keep records…. **SC.K.N.1.4** Observe and create a visual representation…. **SC.K.N.1.5** Recognize that learning can come from careful observation. **SC.K.E.5.1** Explore the Law of Gravity…. **SC.K.E.5.2** Recognize… day and night. **SC.K.E.5.4** Observe that sometimes the Moon can be seen at night and sometimes during the day. **SC.K.E.5.5** Observe that things can be big and things can be small as seen from Earth. **SC.K.E.5.6** Observe that some objects are far away and some are nearby as seen from Earth. (TE)

moon

Draw.

At night we may see stars in the sky.
On most nights we see the moon.

▶ Draw the moon.

Name _____

We may also see the moon during the day.

Name _____

Sum It Up!

● Draw the day sky.   ▲ Draw the night sky.

Matter

matter

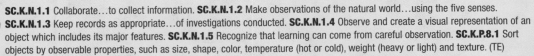

SC.K.N.1.1 Collaborate…to collect information. **SC.K.N.1.2** Make observations of the natural world…using the five senses. **SC.K.N.1.3** Keep records as appropriate…of investigations conducted. **SC.K.N.1.4** Observe and create a visual representation of an object which includes its major features. **SC.K.N.1.5** Recognize that learning can come from careful observation. **SC.K.P.8.1** Sort objects by observable properties, such as size, shape, color, temperature (hot or cold), weight (heavy or light) and texture. (TE)

liquid

gas

solid

Matter is anything that takes up space.
Matter can be a liquid, a gas, or a solid.

▶ Draw an X on the liquid.

Name _____

different sizes

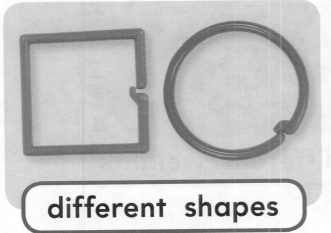

different shapes

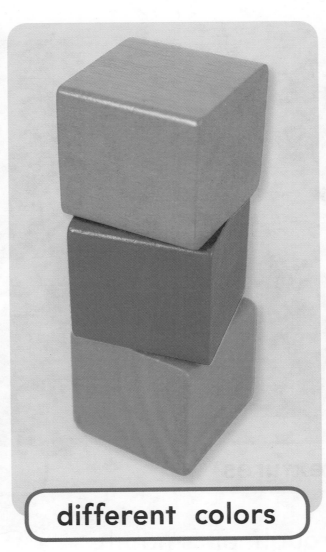

different colors

Objects are different sizes, shapes, and colors.

▶ Draw an object you can tell about.

Name _____

different textures

different weights

Objects may be rough or smooth.
Objects may be heavy or light.

▶ Circle the object that is rough.

Name _____

different temperatures

Draw.

Things may be hot or cold.

▶ Draw a cold drink you like.

Sum It Up!

  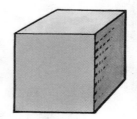 

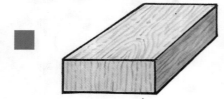 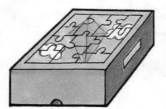  

- ● Circle the object that is a different color.
- ▲ Circle the object that is a different size.
- ■ Circle the object that is a different shape.

Matter Can Change

change

© Houghton Mifflin Harcourt Publishing Company

SC.K.N.1.1 Collaborate with a partner to collect information. **SC.K.N.1.2** Make observations of the natural world and know that they are descriptors collected using the five senses. **SC.K.N.1.3** Keep records as appropriate...of investigations conducted. **SC.K.N.1.4** Observe and create a visual representation of an object which includes its major features. **SC.K.N.1.5** Recognize that learning can come from careful observation. **SC.K.P.9.1** Recognize that the shape of materials such as paper and clay can be changed by cutting, tearing, crumpling, smashing, or rolling. (TE)

Name _____

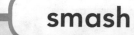
tear

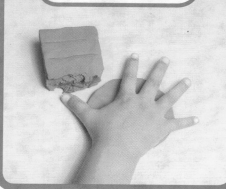

smash

roll

bend

Draw.

We can change clay.

▶ Draw something you can make from clay.

Name _____

cut

fold

crumple

We can change paper.

▶ Circle the paper being cut.

Sum It Up!

●

▲

■

● Circle the paper that is cut.   Circle the paper that is folded.
■ Circle the clay that is smashed.

Heating and Cooling Matter

heat

cool

SC.K.N.1.1 Collaborate…to collect information. **SC.K.N.1.2** Make observations of the natural world…using the five senses. **SC.K.N.1.3** Keep records as appropriate…. **SC.K.N.1.4** Observe and create a visual representation of an object…. **SC.K.N.1.5** Recognize that learning can come from careful observation. **SC.K.P.8.1** Sort objects by observable properties, such as size, shape, color, temperature (hot or cold), weight (heavy or light) and texture. (TE)

heating

✏️ Draw.

raw egg

cooked egg

Matter may change when it heats up.

▶ Draw a cooked egg.

Name _____

liquid

cooling

solid

When matter cools, it may change.
A liquid may become a solid.

▶ Circle the matter being cooled.

Unit 5 • Lesson 19 •
How Can Heating and Cooling Change Matter?

81

Name _____

Sum It Up!

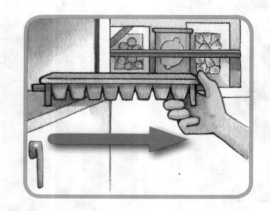  

Unit 5 • Lesson 19 •
How Can Heating and Cooling Change Matter?

● Circle what happens when water is cooled.
▲ Circle what happens when pancake batter is heated.

Sound

sound

vibrate

 SC.K.N.1.1 Collaborate with a partner to collect information. **SC.K.N.1.2** Make observations of the natural world and know that they are descriptors collected using the five senses. **SC.K.N.1.3** Keep records as appropriate — such as pictorial records — of investigations conducted. **SC.K.N.1.4** Observe and create a visual representation of an object which includes its major features. **SC.K.N.1.5** Recognize that learning can come from careful observation. **SC.K.P.10.1** Observe that things that make sound vibrate. (TE)

soft

loud

Draw.

Things vibrate back and forth.
This makes a sound.
Sounds may be loud or soft.

▶ Draw something that makes a loud sound.

Name _____

low

high

Draw.

Sounds may be low or high.
What makes a very low sound?

▶ Draw something that makes a high sound.

Name _____

Sum It Up!

● Circle the person making a soft sound.
▲ Circle the person making a low sound.

Light

light

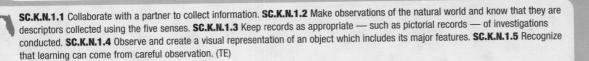

SC.K.N.1.1 Collaborate with a partner to collect information. **SC.K.N.1.2** Make observations of the natural world and know that they are descriptors collected using the five senses. **SC.K.N.1.3** Keep records as appropriate — such as pictorial records — of investigations conducted. **SC.K.N.1.4** Observe and create a visual representation of an object which includes its major features. **SC.K.N.1.5** Recognize that learning can come from careful observation. (TE)

Name _____

sun

lamp

Draw.

flashlight

The sun gives off light.
Some things people make give off light.
Name some things that give off light.

▶ Draw something that gives off light.

Name _____

very little light

a lot of light

We need light to see things.

▶ Circle the room with more light.

Name _____

Sum It Up!

Unit 6 • Lesson 21 •
What Is Light?

Circle the things that give off light.

Heat

heat

 SC.K.N.1.1 Collaborate with a partner to collect information. **SC.K.N.1.2** Make observations of the natural world and know that they are descriptors collected using the five senses. **SC.K.N.1.3** Keep records as appropriate — such as pictorial records — of investigations conducted. **SC.K.N.1.4** Observe and create a visual representation of an object which includes its major features. **SC.K.N.1.5** Recognize that learning can come from careful observation. (TE)

Name _____

toaster

Some things give off heat.

clothes dryer

Unit 6 • Lesson 22 •
What Is Heat?

▶ Circle the thing that uses heat to toast bread.

Name _____

sun

candle

Draw.

Many things give off both heat and light.

▶ Draw something that gives off heat and light.

Name _____

Sound, light, and heat are kinds of energy.
Energy can make things change.

► Circle the sources of sound, light, or heat energy.

Name _____

Sound energy helps you hear.
Light energy helps you see.
Heat energy keeps you warm.

▶ Circle the sources of sound, light, or heat energy.

Name _____

Sum It Up!

    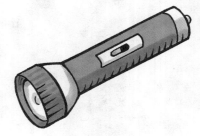

● Circle the thing that gives off light. ▲ Circle the thing that makes sound. ■ Circle the thing that gives off heat.

Where Things Are

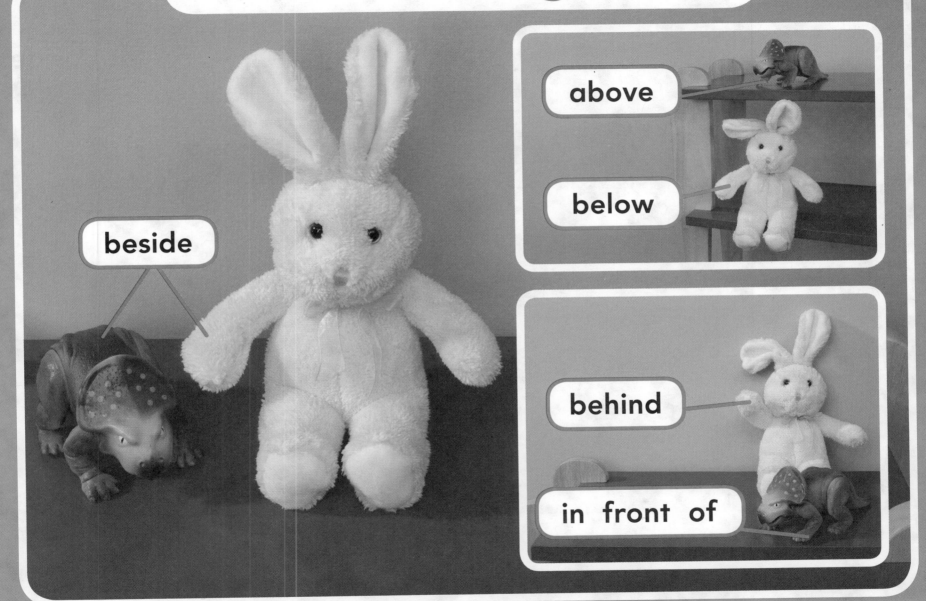

beside

above

below

behind

in front of

SC.K.N.1.1 Collaborate with a partner to collect information. **SC.K.N.1.2** Make observations of the natural world and know that they are descriptors collected using the five senses. **SC.K.N.1.3** Keep records as appropriate — such as pictorial records — of investigations conducted. **SC.K.N.1.4** Observe and create a visual representation of an object which includes its major features. **SC.K.N.1.5** Recognize that learning can come from careful observation. (TE)

Name _____

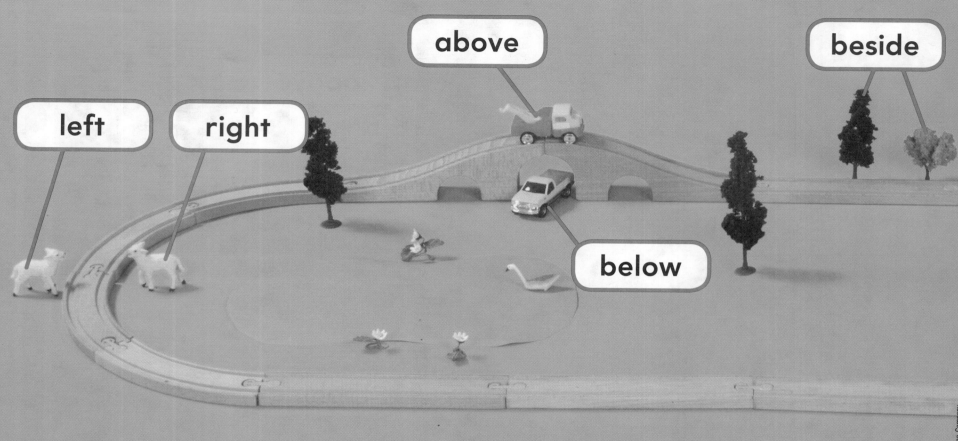

above

beside

left

right

below

You can use words to tell where things are.

Unit 7 • Lesson 23 •
How Do We Describe Location?

▶ Circle the truck below the bridge.

Name _____

in

out

in front of   behind

Where are the ducks?

Draw.

▶ Draw a ball with a tree behind it.

Name _____

Sum It Up!

Color the toy above the airplane yellow. Color the toy below the truck blue. Color the toy beside the ball green. Color the toy in front of the basket orange.

How Things Move

zigzag

round and round

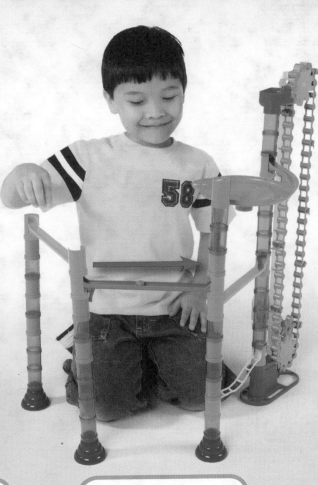

straight

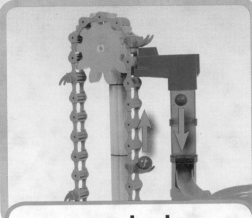

up and down

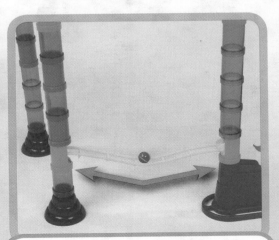

back and forth

SC.K.N.1.1 Collaborate with a partner to collect information. **SC.K.N.1.2** Make observations of the natural world and know that they are descriptors collected using the five senses. **SC.K.N.1.3** Keep records as appropriate — such as pictorial records — of investigations conducted. **SC.K.N.1.4** Observe and create a visual representation of an object which includes its major features. **SC.K.N.1.5** Recognize that learning can come from careful observation. **SC.K.P.12.1** Investigate that things move in different ways, such as fast, slow, etc. (TE)

Name _____

straight

round and round

Things move in different ways.

▶ Color the arrows to show the direction things are moving.

Name _____

up and down

back and forth

zigzag

Things may change direction.

► Color the arrows to show the direction things are moving.

Name _____

fast

Sometimes things move fast.

▶ Draw an X on the animal that can move fast.

Name _____

slow

Sometimes things move slowly.

 Draw.

Sometimes things move slowly.

▶ Draw something that moves slowly.

Sum It Up!

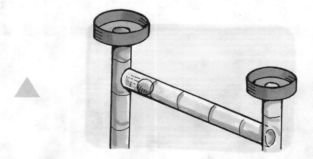  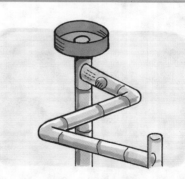

● Circle the train that goes straight. ▲ Circle the marble that goes round and round. ■ Circle the animal that moves slowly.

Changing How Things Move

push

pull

SC.K.N.1.1 Collaborate...to collect information. **SC.K.N.1.2** Make observations.... **SC.K.N.1.3** Keep records....
SC.K.N.1.4 Observe and create a visual representation.... **SC.K.N.1.5** Recognize that learning can come from careful
observation. **SC.K.E.5.1** Explore the Law of Gravity by investigating how objects are pulled toward the ground unless
something holds them up. **SC.K.P.13.1** Observe that a push or a pull can change the way an object is moving. (TE)

Name _____

push

pull

We can push and pull things.
We can change the direction things move.

Unit 7 • Lesson 25 •
How Can We Change the Way Things Move?

▶ Circle the person pulling something.

Name _____

gravity

Gravity pulls things down unless something holds them up.

▶ Draw an arrow to show where the ball will go.

Sum It Up!

How Can We Change the Way Things Move?

● Circle the person pushing.
▲ Circle the person pulling.

Magnets

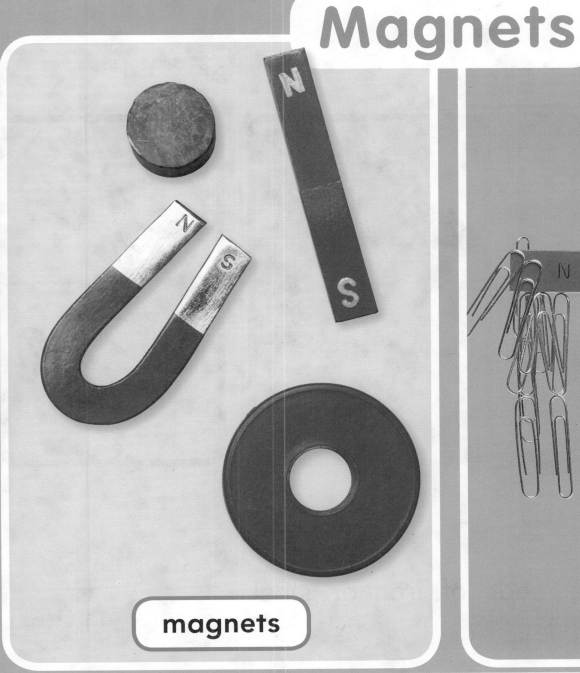

magnets

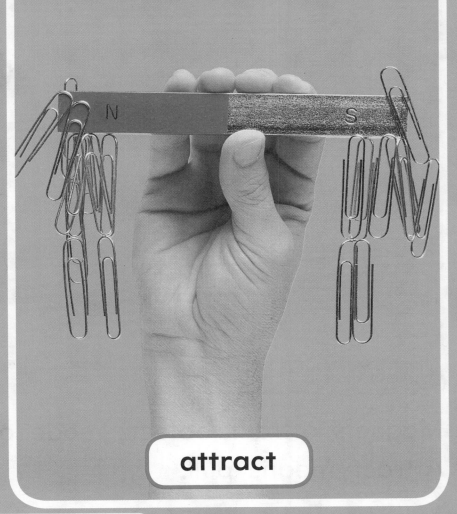

attract

SC.K.N.1.1 Collaborate with a partner to collect information. **SC.K.N.1.2** Make observations of the natural world and know that they are descriptors collected using the five senses. **SC.K.N.1.3** Keep records as appropriate — such as pictorial records — of investigations conducted. **SC.K.N.1.4** Observe and create a visual representation of an object which includes its major features. **SC.K.N.1.5** Recognize that learning can come from careful observation. **SC.K.P.13.1** Observe that a push or a pull can change the way an object is moving. (TE)

Name _____

attract

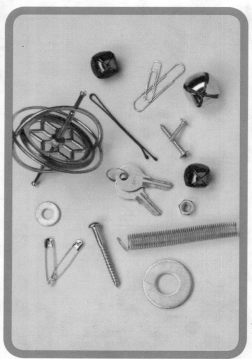

Magnets attract objects made of iron or steel.
Attract means pull.

Unit 7 • Lesson 26 •
Which Objects Do Magnets Attract?

▶ Circle the group of objects a magnet will attract.

Name _____

magnet

✏ Draw.

Magnets can move some objects without touching them.

▶ Draw an arrow to show the direction the truck is moving.

Sum It Up!

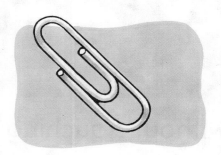  

Unit 7 • Lesson 26 •
Which Objects Do Magnets Attract?

● ▲ ■ Circle the object a magnet will attract.